To every thing there is a season,
and a time to every purpose under
the heaven:
A time to be born, and a time to die; a
time to plant, and a time to pluck up that
which is planted.

— Ecclesiastes 3:1-2

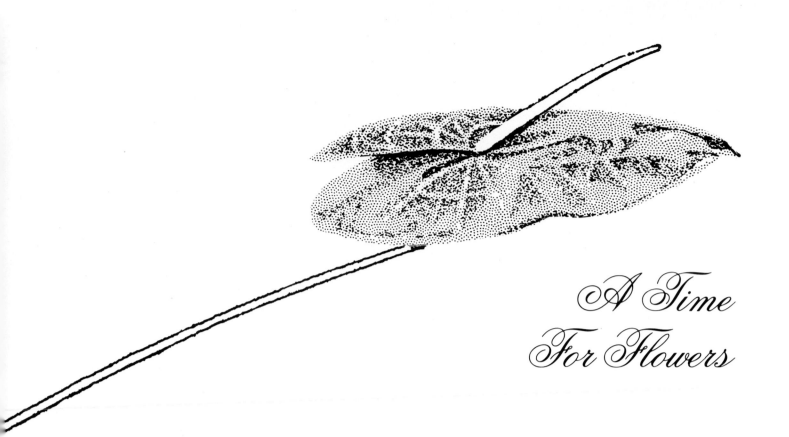

A Time
For Flowers

A Time For Flowers

Dale L. Rohman

Photography by Leonard Lujan

The Patrice Press
Gerald, Missouri

Library of Congress Cataloging in Publication Data

Rohman, Dale L., 1938-
    A Time For Flowers.

    1. Flower arrangement — Pictorial works.
I. Lujan, Leonard.   II. Title.
SB449.R6336   1982   745.92   82-14362
ISBN 0-935284-26-5

Published by
The Patrice Press
Box 42   Gerald, MO 63037

Printed and bound in Japan

To my father,
who gave me a piece of ground behind
the garage when I was very little, and told
me I could plant anything I wanted, and was
never disappointed when it didn't turn out
to be tomatoes.

To my mother,
who always received the bouquets from
my garden as if they were the most precious
flowers on earth,

and to my wife,
who continues to encourage me to do
the thing I enjoy most, even though it takes
a great deal of my time and attention.

Foreword

My first conscious exposure to the art of flower arranging took place at Taliesin, where I was an apprentice to Frank Lloyd Wright. The great room there was dressed for some sort of function. I was puzzled by the giant asymmetrical arrangements of flowering branches and foliage, so I systematically shoved all the arrangements tightly into the vases, as I had seen done with roses and all other flowers until then.

Mr. Wright exploded when he saw the desecration I had wrought. From that moment on, we were all exposed to the art of flower arranging — not as taught in the conventional Japanese or classical schools, but in accordance with the universal principles of design. Foremost among the considerations was the respect for the character of each flower, each leaf, and each branch. We had to arrange them to highlight their natural and distinctive beauty. I have never forgotten those lessons, but one is rarely exposed to such sensitivity these days.

So I was both surprised and delighted to see those same principles espoused by Frank Lloyd Wright being practiced on a day-to-day basis by Dale Rohman. He incorporates his own perceptivity and sensitive awareness to each background and setting.

He practices almost exclusively in St. Louis, but his artistry would be at home in Bombay or Fleet Street or in the opera house in Sydney. I shouldn't say his creations have a stunning beauty as do, say, some examples of the architectural arts. Rather, they have an enveloping sense of being. Like the very aroma of the media, they approach the viewer with delicacy and grace (and sometimes outrageous whimsy). When all is said and done, we gaze in some sort of rapture at what Dale Rohman has wrought.

I am both pleased and flattered that I have been chosen to prepare the foreword for this book. I do so not to help Dale Rohman gain the popular accolades he so richly deserves, but as a simple tribute from one artist to another.

William A. Bernoudy

William Adair Bernoudy, F.A.I.A.

Introduction

Flowers, to me, are constant evidence that there is beauty around us whenever we need it, and that it comes from someone far greater than we are. No matter where destiny takes us, the sight of even a lowly fleabane in bloom proves that we do have love in our lives, along with beauty, joy, cheer, thoughtfulness, friendship, caring, and all the other emotional bouyants we need in abundant supply.

I have had a garden since those days long ago when my father provided me with my very first one. It has been almost a compulsion. Every year it must be more striking than the last. As each annual display provided greater dimensions in beauty, it became more and more evident that my avocation must be along those lines. I rooted myself in the floral industry because that is what I enjoy doing more than anything in this world; I could have succeeded in doing nothing else.

I suppose that would have been enough; indeed I was grateful that there had been that much for me. But as my time immersed in this ''hobby'' grew from an hour or two to anywhere from 12 to 16 hours a day, there was a natural gravitation toward the creative use of those flowers, to see how they would look in context with other blooms, twigs, buds, containers, and even just plain roadside wildflowers. Without realizing it at the time, my hobby changed from propagation to the art of flower arranging.

Flower arranging is an art form in every sense of the word; to me it is in a leading position in the decorative arts. It is a lot more than flinging flowers in a vase; it is a peerless, individual and personal art form. It is unique because the artist is privileged to work with a medium that in itself is art. Each flower, after all, is an individual creation intrinsic in its perfection, superbly colored, exquisitely its own.

The art form is more than a livelihood for me; it is more than a privilege. It is an awesome gift, even though I worked hard for it. I shall never cease being grateful for having been allowed the opportunity to excel in it.

I once was chided by a friend that my ''so-called art'' was only art of the moment. She said, ''Your posies don't last.'' Certainly the medium is perishable, but in the heart of the recipient the intent of the art lingers forever.

The unique nature of the art form is not its perishability, but the very different-ness of each arrangement. No arrangement can be duplicated exactly, for like snowflakes, no two flowers are exactly alike. Arrangements may be similar to the eye, but each design is always new and fresh.

If the floral artist is to be a creative success, his work must take on a personality. Not that of the artist, as in the case of the other decorative arts, but rather that of the individual for whom the art is created. For some clients I feel the need to express whimsy, for they are humorous and entertaining people. For the giant risk-takers of our community of clientele I try to create a bold presentation. For those who have dramatic personalities I concentrate on creating flamboyant arrange-ments. For the calm and gentle hostess, the art reflects serenity. What results must always be art, to be sure, but it is good art only if it reflects the personality of the client; not that of the artist.

I haven't stopped growing in this art form and I will never allow myself to do so. For in it there is a constant excitement fed by the need to keep apace of our ever changing life styles. Something or someone always sparks a new idea or revamps an old one. The creative juices are ever flowing, feeding the imagination, encourag-ing the slightest whim to sprout wings and fly to artistic reality. My last thoughts before going to sleep every night are of it. I spring from bed daily with a feeling of exhilaration, knowing that this day I shall be able to create anew, to rise to the challenges of the medium.

I don't mean to imply that a floral creation springs forth in a blinding flash. Thomas Edison's quote about his success being 99 percent perspiration is not inappropriate to my art form. There is a great deal of advance preparation needed to complete a ''Picasso in posies.'' The creative moments are altogether too brief; the conception and the touching up sometimes take hours. By most standards I suppose it would be considered work; it just doesn't seem like it.

The rewards of flower arranging need not be confined within the walls of a retail shop, or even within the vast international network of garden clubs and highly specialized schools. Everyone who dabbles in flowers, including and especially those who pick from their own garden and arrange at their kitchen sink, is entitled to share in the joy of considering their flowerpiece as an artifact, a composition designed to blend with or even dominate their own decor.

In fact, those of us who are professionals in the field must admit that the genesis of today's theory, ''less is more,'' is at the hands of the do-it-yourself florist at home. Their push for arrangements that look as if ''I did it myself'' has indeed nourished our efforts to elevate our product from something that sells flowers to an art object which deserves our pride.

I could write on and on about flowers, elaborating on their amusing legends, spilling the sentiment of the once highly practiced Victorian language of flowers, countering the accusation that they are a luxury item only, and providing a colossal list of occasions for their bestowment. (The best reason for giving flowers is no reason at all.) I could explain how a single flower can say a thousand words, how a flower doesn't have to be a pedigreed hothouse bloom to be beautiful — the lowly roadside fleabane, again, is a case in point. But the thought I most want to convey is the simple notion that flowers are for everyone. The beauty of their brief lives mirrors the beauty in our long ones, whether they grow in my garden or yours.

The arrangements in this book were created for some very special people. They are prominent in the social, cultural and artistic world of St. Louis. They have lent their home settings; their decorative containers, accessories and backgrounds; and most important, their own personalities to the assemblage of these examples of individual flower arrangements.

Many of these clients went to great lengths to cooperate, permitting us to invade their privacy, to rearrange their furniture, to work sometimes as late as midnight until we had achieved the results we wanted.

Many others were helpful in acting as intermediaries with those in charge of organizations and public places used as backgrounds for some of these arrangements. The patience and gracious assistance of these important and busy people is indeed appreciated.

''You must lie awake at night coming up with your ideas,'' a customer once told me. Not so. The art form is demanding but it is also fulfilling. I sleep the sleep of the sated.

— Dale L. Rohman
August 31, 1982

Acknowledgments

As I'm about to express my sincere appreciation to the many friends who have so unselfishly helped me put my book together and make my dream come true, I can't help but remember good old Murray Fink.

Murray and I once worked together for Dorothy and Leland Gillette at Parkview Gardens Florist in St. Charles, Missouri. I used to call him the ''15-year-old, red-headed, freckle-faced, Lutheran preacher boy.'' To be a Lutheran minister was his goal in life (which he has achieved) and he sincerely felt the only way to heaven was through the Lutheran gates. Anyway, one day Leland sent Murray to the Catholic church with flowers and explicit instructions to place them on the altar of the Blessed Virgin. Some time later the priest discovered Murray wandering aimlessly and confused through his church. 'May I help you, young man?'' asked the priest. ''I hope so,'' Murray answered desperately. ''I'm supposed to give these flowers to someone but I've forgotten the lady's name!''

I don't want to forget any names, but if I do, I hope those so injured will be as understanding as Leland was with Murray — gentle, kind and unflappable.

I'll begin with my gratitude to Reg Petty and Wood Livingstone of Pettymark for their generous contribution to the ''Black-tie Picnic'' layout — china, crystal, flatware, napkins and even the black ties.

I think special praise is in order for the artistic talent of Marietta Duntz, who deftly penned the anthurium drawings at the beginning of the book.

I can't say enough good things about my long time buddy, ''Uncle'' Gus Beiser. He, along with Raymond Masek Florist, donated the 150 beautiful Samantha roses which were photographed for the Powell Hall layout.

I also want to express thanks to Marianne O'Neal of Busch's Grove for her kind assistance on the Omega night of our photography sessions.

To Clarissa Start I express a whole bouquet of thanks for helping pick and bunch my prose.

A friend indeed is Candace Mundt, who pitched in at the very birth of this dream. Besides being responsible for a great deal of research, telephone calls and secretarial work, she was honest with me when honesty was what I really needed.

I wish I could say more than thanks to Greg Franzwa. He opened a whole new experience to me in the sharing of his art.

Moritz Fuchs, my business partner and the co-owner of George Waldbart Floral Company, deserves and certainly receives my utmost gratitude. His unending patience was surpassed only by his mechanical talents and his willingness to let me share both of them.

A Time
For Flowers

Mrs. Henry G. Keeler Jr.

Above and overleaf: A handsome collection of
Steuben glass provides both the inspiration and the
the appointments for this arrangement, placed in an
entrance hall. Dark, velvety iris tower over emerald
ripple peperomia plants, while white and purple
African violets harmonize in moss at the base of the
arrangement. Note that the exploding flower design
in the wallpaper in the background accepts the
superimposition of the flower creation in the fore-
ground. The entire dioramic composition has a
dreamy, airy feeling, as if you could walk — or
float — right through it.

Mrs. H. Ivis Johnsto

His Imperial Highness, Prince Pu Lun of China, presented this container to Mrs. Johnston's great-grandfather, William H. Thompson, treasurer of the great Louisiana Purchase Exhibition of 1904. Made in the style of Kiung-Lung-Kiln, an emperor who was a patron of the arts, it was 340 years old at the time the gift was given. It even survived the Boxer Rebellion.

The vase on the living room mantle holds stately magnolia. Its glossy green leaves, rusty felted beneath, reign over the orna mental foliage of croton and the serpentined vines of bittersw
Appropriately, the history of the magnolia stems from China, It is believed that the tree was cultivated, not for the beauty of its blooms, but for the aphrodisiac quality of its powdered bar

Mrs. J. Ford Armstrong III

A cantaloupe is the container for a Janet Craig Compacta dracaena plant, creating a pineapple lookalike. A coconut holds a Rosette sansevieria. And a grotesque horseradish root is the receptacle for a serene bloom of narcissus. The root was cut off at the base and inverted. The base of the root form is exposed for the interest of its texture. A container of orange lilies is in the background, as seen in the photo at left.

Above: A combination of plants and edibles is unconventional, perhaps, and yet can be artistic. The diverse elements are unified by the beauty of form they share.

Mrs. Zane E. Barnes

Crystal vases, necklaced in fine gold cord, carry the supreme elegance of gardenias. The tree branch effect in the center vase is fashioned from sheet moss and spathiphyllum foliage.

White flowers were used to highlight a white, black and brown effect, a combination which imparts an Oriental feeling, in conformity with the interesting table, chairs and wallpaper.

The plain gold band of Buckingham by Minton promises a dinner as dramatic as the setting.

Mrs. Ethan A. H. Shepley Jr.

A sampler of the autumn harvest is gathered in these beautifully patterned antique baskets. Posing in arrested gaiety are eggplants and artichokes, small red Holland peppers, fruited crabapple, spathiphyllum foliage, money eucalyptus, and the daisy-like chrysanthemum, Red Rover.

They are pieced together in the same vibrant, vivid colors as the quilt.

The quilt is in the "Texas Star" pattern and is one of a collection used as wall hangings. It is believed to be as old as the 100-year-old farmhouse in which it hangs.

Mrs. Michael E. Pulitzer

Above: An oil painting by the St. Louis artist, E. Oscar Thalinger (1885-1965) dominates this eclectic collection of notable art on a living room mantel. Its subtle touch of red sets the color theme.

Topiary trees of galax leaves with Sincerity red geranium blossoms balance on stems of corkscrew willow. They are based in early American silver candlesticks. They hover over figurines of Shakespeare and Milton by Thomas Parr, Staffordshire factory, c. 1840.

Red geraniums, while unknown in the time of Milton and Shakespeare, flourished in English gardens during the reign of Queen Victoria. Their brilliant color matched that of the uniforms of the queen's guards.

The mask in the center of the mantel is African, the plates on either side, Chinese export porcelain, Chien Lung c. 1748.

Right: This arrangement is created with anthurium foliage, dusty pink carnations and heather, united in a splashed Chien vase by David Morris. The drawing enhancing the flowers is by Luis Caballero.

Mrs. Donald N. Brandin

"Encore wedding" is the name being given to a second marriage. For this one, three natural ficus trees, each almost eight feet tall, are adorned with rubrum lilies and baby's breath. Cut Oregon ferns flourish at their base.

The eye is directed upward by pastel ribbons knotted and attached to the trunk of each tree. These echo the tiny streamers fastened to the wedding invitations.

KILLED
OCT 24, 1948
HEARSCH'S WOODS
BRIDLESPUR HUNT

Mrs. Wm. Maffitt Bates Jr.

Preceding page: An incredible bounty of watermelons, ornamental peppers, sword leaf eucalyptus, variegated tree ivy, anthurium foliage, dried achillea (yarrow) and Rieger begonia blossoms overflow from an early 19th century silver container acquired at the Chinese Pavilion of the 1904 Louisiana Purchase Exposition.

Right: A half watermelon becomes a vessel for more Rieger begonias, ficus foliages and a portion of melon. The astute observer will note one slice has been sampled. The broken ostrich egg is the source of an omelet cooked by the renowned St. Louis Zoo director, George Vierheller.

Right and below: Trophies have been decorated for fun — begonia blossoms and miniature red peppers join in with Charleston popcorn wreaths — sold on the roadsides of South Carolina. They are made of wild popcorn — really wild, for it pops when brought into a warm room. The ribbons — Gucci.

Mrs. Eugene F. Williams Jr.

Dual rings of ivy intertwine with defoliated honeysuckle vines, heather and alstroemeria blossoms. They are housed in a pair of matching cache pots. The alstroemeria is a flower of the Peruvian lily family. Rubrum lilies skyrocket from the axis of symmetry to celebrate the painting, *Les Feuillages,* by Larinov, c. 1905.

Mrs. Van-Lear Black II.

Whimsy is broad based on an intriguing hippopotamu collection

Top left: The mossed hippo at right carries creeping fig emblazoned by several hyacinth blossoms. Another carrie an azalea topiary tree while still another balances a tower o trained ivy. Smaller figures stand by, mouths agape — per haps shouting a favorite line from The Curious Savage ''Don't forget to take your umbrella.'

Top right: An Aloe vera plant gives a ride to a couple o miniature jonquil blossoms. The hippo front and cente spews King Alfred jonquils while its neighbor produces maypole mirage: ribbons flowing from a single white Rove chrysanthemum

Left: A hippo of voluptuous proportions holds cut flowers a it was designed to do — miniature jonquils called ''tete-a tete'' around a single towering tulip

Right: How sweet it is — ecstasy shared with a ladybug Here is a true exemplification of the advice, ''Don't forge to smell the flowers.'

Mrs. Hugh Scott Jr.

Here is a skylighted greenhouse bathroom, where a collection of plants luxuriates in steamy humidity. A might
weeping fig soars over harmoniously placed Boston fern
caladiums, spathiphyllum and a fiddle leaf fig. A splash o
color is spilled by a calceolaria (pocketbook plant) and tube
ous begonias. A gathering of woven terra cotta containe
perform various functions on the bath ledge. One serves a
a towel holder, another groups bronze colored cineraria
to provide pleasing color harmony with the coppery cr
tons and red-orange pixie gladiolu

Bird at Rest

Leptospermum appears to grow wild behind a contrived miniature woodpile. A bisque Goebel snowbird has come to rest avoiding the flagstones, heavily laden with the brown skins from narcissus bulbs.

Mrs. F. Crunden Cole

Above and left: An interesting ensemble of hand blown glass vases provides both a decorative and practical design — rooting plants. Among the cuttings are a strawberry geranium, spider plant, Chinese evergreen, Rosetta sansevieria and aboricola, which is a form of miniature schefflera. The new fledged sprouts can stand alone as decorative accessories or be enhanced with cut flowers — cyclamen blossoms, freesia, a green spider mum and iris.

Such a windowsill in bloom provides a touch of spring and latches winter out.

Mrs. Stanley Nelson Hollander

Top left: A free flowing mobile of grape ivy weaves through branches of cor screw willow parasites to a wall chandelier in a guest powder room. Ribbo tied, water-filled vials hold sweethearts (Golden Garnet), fragrant na cissus poeticus and foliage nipped from a strawberry geraniur

Top: The Meissen compote, of German porcelain, with pierced latti work and heavily encrusted flowers and cherubs, once was part of the Rot child collection, France, 1803-1850. A touch of bygone opulence is the han made Belgian lace cloth from Bruge

Right: A candelabra effect is achieved by bringing the flowers up to e velop the chandelier. Here is a festive abundance of Japanese iris, rubru and Golden Trumpet lilies, tulips, roses, carnations and acacia. We use sprays of pink silk flowers to harmonize with the fresh. The connectin uninterrupted look provides an elegant table settin

Mrs. William Upthegrove

Here is a living room with an emphasis on color — vibrant color in the print of the sofa, the boldness of the rug, the patent leather look of the chair, even the bulbous bunny whose brassy coating can't conceal the carved wood beneath.

Left: An Alessandra basket holds winter magnolia. The branches were broken by a storm and burned by the wind, but were rescued and lightly spray painted to suggest the patina of the rabbit. Pots of tulips and cineraria establish an indoor garden.

Above: Pots of tulips nest in Spanish moss and a wreath of wild grapevines.

Mrs. Marlon B. Wallace Jr.

Here in the game room is a study in fragile interaction of flora and fauna. Home-grown white camellias are clustered with purple Cineraria to provide a regal environment for the mounted vivid and colorful South African birds, lilac breasted rollers.

Mrs. Lawrence K. Roos

Above: Feather-veined green and white caladium leaves couple with light and airy allium blooms to enhance the elegance of a pristine white bisque swan. A pair of newer swans carries partially reflexed tulips and Tradescantia foliage. Together they glide majestically beneath a print of English songbirds.

Left: The aquatic bird assumes a different aura by moonlight.

Mrs. Donald E. Breckenridge

Preceding page: Dinner for two in the master bedroom calls for something special. The table has been dressed in yellow moire, garlanded in grape ivy, baby's breath and Golden Trumpet lilies. Five hues of ribbon, braided and woven through the garland, pick up the blues and greens of the room's decor. The whippet is rendered in glazed porcelain.

Right: Five candlesticks are used as a centerpiece. Three hold yellow candles. One serves as the base of a mossed topiary, baby ivy curling around its trunk. It is topped by a trumpet lily. The fifth holder contains a stem of trumpet lilies, tied with the five shades of ribbon to repeat the theme found in the table garland, below.

A container of sentimental value produces an unexpected performance by three crisp cabbage-like collards. Among some of their ruffled leaves, the silvery velvet texture of artemisia (dusty miller) may be seen. Others allow the elegant and delicate sprays of dendrobium orchids to soar away.

Perched alone in a crystal cigarette urn, a white Snow Song rose balances the coffee table grouping.

Mrs. William Adair Bernoudy

Left: A Japanese basket is filled, very simply, with tulips, reflexed to show their jet black centers and to give the poppy look beloved by the Flemish masters.

Right: In a hallway beneath a distinguished Siamese Buddha, a clear bottle, designed to hold a single flower, has been purposely over-stuffed with sprays of treated grass. Piggybacked on its squared base are four miniature bottles of the same shape carrying kalanchoe flowerets, an orange lily and one orange Belinda rose.

Mrs. James Lee Johnson Jr.

The masques, themselves hiding in the arrangement, suggest the song title, ''After The Ball.'' Their stage is the table, polished aluminum with its top of solar bronze glass. Only crystal accessories are used on it.

The crystal bubble holds the three masques formed from eucalyptus leaves, their standards serving as stems. Spider plant, a shooting spire of Leptospermum, Boston ferns and wisps of treated grass complete the scene. The masque standards are held in place by shards of a broken mirror, painted black on one side for a dramatic study in contrast.

Colorful Culinaria

The color scheme is bright red and green; the media are vegetables, fruit and fir boughs in silver containers, a silver compote, a silver basket and a silver bonbon dish.

Color is supplied by both the decorative and edible components. Sliced peppers, radishes, reflexed red tulips, red azaleas and the buds from rubrum lily stems add to the flashing display.

Tulips and azalea blossoms are arranged in a fresh pear — that receptacle serves as a fourth container.

Mix with imagination and serve on a round mirror.

Mrs. Richard C. Holton

Three cylinders of crystal, varying in height, support alstroemeria blooms, their stems shored up with sea shells. The burnished blossoms blend with the colors of the shells in the vases and those framing the mirror, a creation of Mary Robertson Jones.

Below: A ruffled clam shell becomes a marina for coral colored Sonia roses anchored by smaller shells.

Mrs. Henry B. Pflager II

The unique vase could never be considered ordinary, but the trans-
formation to aquarium made it extraordinary indeed. A lamp
chimney inside the container keeps the fish in view while a glass
vase inserted in the chimney allows Scotch broom (Cytisus) to
burst geyser-like up and out of the improvised fish bowl. The fish
have their own private arena in front of an animal patterned
Oriental screen.

Mrs. Bourne Bean

A floral covered table announces luncheon for four in a flower-filled gazebo room. Heavily fragrant narcissus blooms are knotted in ribbon streamers (left) and dangle from an amusing black wire cloche. It becomes the centerpiece, which would be *de trop* at table level. Blooming plants from the adjacent greenhouse are placed between the lacy wicker chairs and, as a final floral touch, a fresh narcissus on each salad plate.

Mrs. James T. Chamness

Opposite: This black lacquered Chinese coffee table, inlaid with mother-of-pearl, dates to about 1890. The green glazed clay vase is from the Ming dynasty, 15th-16th centuries.

With this prestigious beginning, appropriately important cymbidium orchids, white-veined mauve in color, provided the central theme of this arrangement. It is highlighted with mauve colored waxflowers and a burst of stemmed ribbon buds.

Above: The rose, queen of flowers and symbol of regal beauty, reigns supreme in the grandeur of a George II silver epergne, c.1757. Seemingly emerging from their own petals, the flowers rule over suspended silver-latticed baskets. Each of those carries a single sweetheart rose nestled among more petals and blossoms of Leptospermum and waxflower. Some have been purposely spilled on the round French Louis XVI satinwood table. It has a spiral parquetry top and edged apron, c.1810.

The tradition of using rose petals originated in ancient Rome, when they were strewn lavishly during processions and banquets. The ostentatious Emperor Heliogabalus (c.205-222) once released so many petals from the ceiling that some of his guests suffocated.

And Cleopatra, legend claims, stuffed her pillows and mattresses with millions of rose petals before beckoning Mark Anthony to her bedside.

Mrs. Robert C. West

The quietness of a single flower, a contrived, man-made bloom of gladiolus petals, takes the form of a camellia and rests atop a bamboo stalk. Named glamellia, the flower on its artificial stem takes protea foliage as its own and comes to rest in a vase shaped by Robert C. West Jr. in the manner of the Celadon ware from Thailand. The Balinese figure and the bronze head of a young Vietnamese woman pose on a rosewood wine cooler from China. The elongated torso was fashioned because the carver, commissioned to do two statues from a single piece of wood, refused to cut such perfection in half and instead created only one slim figure. Providing the background is a hand-carved walnut screen from the Kashmir region of India. All the artifacts were assembled by the Wests during their travels in the Orient.

Mrs. E. Lawrence Keyes Jr.

An assembly of candlesticks surround a cherub-adorned lamp. A single topiary fabricated from the slender silvery-gray foliage of carnations, studded with pink mini carnations and fashioned to a gnarled trunk, stretches from the wings of a bronze stork. The two green-patterned candlesticks are Chinese. One holds a two-tiered topiary of dusty pink carnations, the other a candle decorated with the simplicity of a single flower.

Mrs. Philip B. Cady

"For unto you is born this day in the city of David, a Saviour, which is Christ the Lord." It is an age-old story, ever new. This nativity creche is constructed of wild grape vines and woven with boughs of silver fir. It shelters the white porcelain figures of the Holy Family. Echoing the Christian symbolism of "peace of mind" and "desire for heaven," white hyacinths burst into bloom. The illusionary dogwood tree in the wallpaper background seems to hover over the miracle, patiently awaiting its role in the Christian drama.

Mrs. Edwin S. Jones

A delicate Victorian epergne reflects the family
heritage in a Chippendale mirror. The container has
been a family heirloom for three generations. Its
soft green ruffled trumpets now flourish with
Bridal Pink roses and single flowered geraniums,
garlanded by frail loops of satin ribbon

Liquid Amber

A flea market find, amber colored and violin shaped, once
held spirituous liquid, now contains only water. The bottle
takes on remnants of plant material: leftover pieces of
bittersweet, sprigs of corkscrew willow snipped from
another arrangement, chunks of moss, miscellaneous
grasses and one large begonia leaf. On a graceful piecrust
table, the one-time castoff has itself become an object
of grace.

Mrs. L. Rumsey Ewing

Right: Coral pink anthurium and camellia foliage rise rhythmically from a por celain shell-shaped container, handcrafted by Courtney Bean. They pose before coramandel screen from the Chien Lung dynasty, c. 1736-1795

Somehow reminiscent of adolescence, these flowers with their gangling leg reflect inherent grace. The look is at once severe and precise, yet meltingl appealing

Above: An almost bookless bookcase becomes an ideal niche to house a collectio of exquisite pieces of miniature furniture, handcrafted by retired police an fire chiefs of Ladue. Matching their proportions, miniature perfume bottles becom containers for pinched florets taken from blooming plants: kalanchoe, Persia violets, African violets and begonias

Mr. James A. Van Sant

Mr. Van Sant hosted an elegant dinner at his club in honor of his friend, Miss Beverly Sills. His only stipulation: all flowers must be chrysanthemums. It was a real challenge to create harmony without monotony. Luckily, chrysanthemums themselves are possessed with great variety and, chameleon-like, they take on the look of daisies and dahlias, along with their own pompom, shaggy and bouffant forms.

A continuing runner of flowers down the center of the table lends the feeling of a garden. The clumps of chrysanthemums nestle into grapevines, Spanish moss and oak leaf ivy.

Only two white Rover chrysanthemums were used, both at the place of the distinguished guest of honor.

Overleaf: The display leaves the table to soar into the chandelier.

Mrs. Orrin S. Wightman III

Dinner for eight — a cool medley of green and white. "Black Knight" Bavarian china and French crystal circle an epergne designed for a fresh and natural garden effect. A pie shell of moss nests in the shallow base of the epergne. Rex begonias and variegated ivy are planted there. Cut freesia add additional blooms to the flower bed. The horn of the epergne, holding clear marbles, is crowned with a burst of white cyclamen, an entire plant of it. More freesia breaks away for added height.

Mrs. Monte C. Throdahl

Left: The blue and white tea caddy and teapot were made in Canton for export in 1830, and given to Mrs. Throdahl by an aunt, Mrs. C.E. Mudd, who liked to call Canton "everybody's porcelain."

It has been placed on a sarcophagus-shaped cellaret of of Regency mahogany, made in England about 1810. It is an ideal small coffee table as well as a convenient store-away spot. The Victorian sofa is carved walnut and once belonged to a grandmother in Virginia.

The caddy has been used as a container for a birds nest of honeysuckle, intertwined with tradescantia, Spanish moss, and starred with the blossoms of freesias. The irregular lines of a Christmas cactus contribute an Oriental effect.

Above: A Sheraton ladies' secretary in light mahogany (England, C.1790). The painting, *The Watergate,* is by the western artist, Michael Coleman. The container is blown three-mold glass, made in Boston, probably in the Sandwich glass works, about 1835. Three stems of stock rise from the container. African violets spill from the secretary.

Elevated Eloquence

To heighten a bold and striking appearance, an amaryllis is transplanted into a drain pipe, and saucered in black rock.

Tulipmania

Narcissus bulbs planted atop brightly painted wooden candlesticks
produce brightly colored tulips, the flowers that once captivated
Holland. While some are cupped to focus their warm colors, others
invert their petals in order to spread their hue. Though flashy
en masse, even a single column can be showy.

Mrs. John Brodhead Jr.

Left: A continuous flow of foliage encircles and embraces a mantel which holds an assemblage of antiques. On the flanks are a pair of 19th century four-branched ormulu and onyx girandoles. Between them and the clock are a pair of early 20th century Chinese vases, footed and lidded. All are nestled in rhythms of Douglas fir boughs, honeysuckle vines, galax leaves, carnation foliage, dried baby's breath and Spanish moss. Orange Enchantment lilies add a lively accent.

Only three persimmon colored candles grace the candelabra — the fourth and center holder is crowded with added Enchantment lilies.

Mrs. Joseph G. Werner

Above: A coffee table is the base for a bucolic gathering. Pottery an
bronze farm animals mosey around a wooden crate which serves as
pseudo pasture. Non-flowering kalanchoe, angel plant succulents an
white majestic daisies rise in shimmering contrast as the goose stare
in wonderment

Right: An antique English leather bucket bears an oversize Boston fer
tree with a garden at its feet: hyacinths, grape ivy and lacopodium
Although only one tree is in view, the room houses a pair, each situate
on matching Chippendale chests and backed by matching Italian mirror
The Russian bronze sculpture is by Alexander Lancerat

Mrs. John S. Childress

Left: This prize winning pottery container is an heirloom of the future. Handcrafted by Shelley Childress, it is belted with a cord of jute and airily filled with aralia and peacock feathers. It salutes a serene flight of stuffed canvasback, merganser, mallard and wood ducks. A second Childress crock is topped with African violets.

Right: Two pottery jugs — rough, almost tweedy and herringbone in texture, are also tomorrow's heirlooms. These were created by Bixby Childress. They are enhanced by a branch from a maple tree, purposely twisted. Three soft and delicate ranunculus flowers provide contrast. This arrangement illustrates the artistic value of understatement.

Mrs. Edward J. Schnuck

A look of opulence comes from the ornately gold leafed marble top French table. It is further embellished by an Austrian urn filled with artfully looped myrtle foliage, pittosporum, and deep pink ivy geranium, falling from beneath the blades of pink gladiolus.

Above: Red Swedish ivy, lacopodium, galax leaves, hot pink kalanchoe and magnificently abundant sprays of miniature cymbidium orchids overflow a French dore oval container.

Checkmate

Bottles have become chessmen, grouped on the wooden board.
Miniature beverage bottles divide into two teams, the browns and
the clears. The flowers are the same in each. The paper white
narcissus are pawns, the rose is queen, a nerine lily is king.
Cyclamen, miniature carnations and alstroemeria form the other
warriors. A game is actually in progress.

Mrs. W. Boardman Jones J[...]

Spilling from a handpainted soup tureen imported from China in 181[...] white Leptospermum, yellow acacia, red tulips and yellow jonquils illu[...] trate how one arrangement may be made acceptable in two different setting[...]

Above: On a chest in the living room, beneath an ancestral portrait, th[...] composition appears massive, yet retains a delicate and airy feelin[...]

Right: On a sideboard in the dining room the display loses its massiv[...] look to fade into and become part of the wallpape[...]

The Saint Louis Art Museum

James D. Burke, Director

Bare branches, sprays of eucalyptus and white flowering Amelanchier provide short flowing lines to the massive fountain in Sculpture Hall. Color is contributed by alstroemeria, seafoam statice, gerbera daisies and carnations — together they create impressionism in bloom.

Mrs. C.C. Johnson Spink

There's a garden on the corner, the corner of the desk of the mayor of the City of Ladue. Wicker bread baskets are planted informally with cheerful red caladiums, pink hyacinths and pink ranunculus. They are given greenery by variegated ivy and Chlorophytum comosum — the spider plant.

Mrs. John W. Hanley

A Fourth of July in flowers is formed by an overflowing abundance of multi
colored ranunculus. They are in a huge seashell mounted on a lucite base
and enliven a lonely summer fireplace. There may be no heat, but there i
a lot of warmth

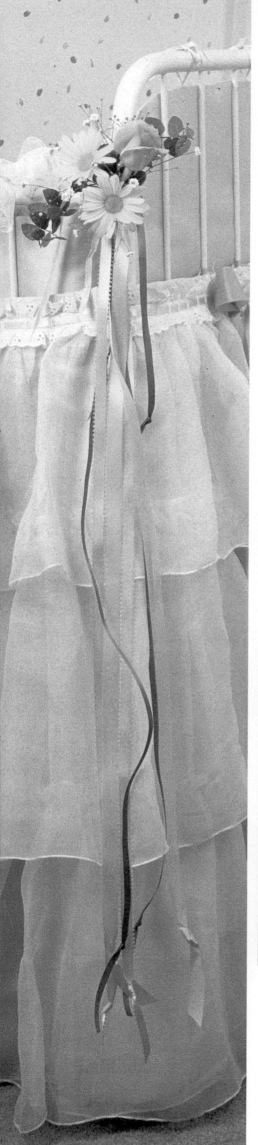

Mrs. J. Curtis Engler

Here is a living mobile of fresh flowers — yellow daisies, pink hyacinth blossoms and creeping fig foliage. It is designed to fascinate baby on Christening Day. A large papier mache butterfly provides beguiling motion. Clusters of pink sweetheart roses and yellow daisies are tied to the bed with long ribbon streamers. The crib has cuddled babies in this family for three generations.

Mrs. Joseph H. White

Above and top right: Bare branches are forced into bloom with the attachment of miniature red carnations and galax leaves. Toy soldiers and American flags among red caladium leaves add a patriotic flare.

Above right: Additional red- and green-leaved caladium plants provide a perfect foil for the plaid.

Mrs. H. Leighton Morrill

A china wicker market basket overflows with galax leaves, green pears, strawberries and Granny Smith apples. The "laundry baskets" on the sides support pineapple-shaped Janet Craig Compacta dracaena, which echo the fruit motif.

On a nearby sideboard, beneath the ancestral portrait of Sally Carter O'Fallon, lattice porcelain cache pots contain lively red azaleas called Chimes.

Mrs. Richard F. Ford

Branches of pink weigela lazily stretch from a terra cotta basket adding
a glow to the already intense sunny colors of a sun room. Overhead, Boston
ferns burst from hanging baskets, where hot pink spikes of Leptospermum
force their way upward into the airspace. Pink and white astilbe stalks
rise from the floor, peeking into the room from behind the Saarinen table
in the corner.

Greenberg Gallery of Contemporary Art

RONALD GREENBERG

Above: An expressionistic head, a painted bronze sculpture by Roy Lichtenstein, is made even more striking by the repetition of its own colors in flowers — lilies of orange, yellow and apricot. The container is a basic one, a simple bushel basket sprayed matte black.

Left: The acrylic on canvas by Jules Olinski is entitled *Hochmel's Voyage.* It is behind a bronze table by Diego Giacomatti. A Japanese storage jar of the Tambawna Momajama period, clay with brown purple glaze, serves as a springboard for the graceful dominance of dogwood.

Mrs. Jackson C. Parriott

A giraffe figurine resting on the spiral staircase seems to be protecting the vase of
fluffy viburnum. (Most people know them by the affectionate name of ''snowballs.''
Their impudent companions are yellow and chartreuse zinnias — made of paper

Opera Theatre of St. Louis

RICHARD GADDES, DIRECTOR

Here is an aria of African protea, branches of Spanish moss, eucalyptus, pink alstroemeria, red gerbera daisies, dried and dyed pink seed tassels and chartreuse sprays of ''kangaroo paws.'' They harmonize to heighten the excitement of opening night, and their contrasting elements reflect the variety of the season's program.

Mrs. Robert R. Hermann

Top: A wedding rehearsal dinner under the big top. Festive flowery chintz cloths made especially for the occasion allow a repeat of coloration in an exuberant mass of flowers — orange lilies, orange gerbera, Queen Anne's lace, Sonia roses with purple and red fushcias and sprengeri foliage.

Opposite, far left: The trunk of the flowery tree is covered with overlapped galax leaves.

Opposite, top right: A reflection of the arrangement was created by removing the five-branch top of the silver candelabra and placing it on a miniature version of the galax tree trunk with just a few flowers tucked in.

Above: Even the fountain in the center of the patio flows flowers — blue hydrangea, red and orange geraniums, pumpkin-hued kalanchoe, with additional droplets of fuchsias.

Opposite bottom: A swan tureen bubbles on the bridal table with a mixture of the same flowers.

Mrs. Robert R. Hermann

Right: A topiary tree of eucalyptus, ivy and miniature schefflera foliage bloom
with the vivid, strong colors of zinnias, iris, miniature carnations and gerbe
daisies. It springs from a terra cotta rabb

Left: In contrast to the formal dining room, the table centerpieces are an inform
repeat of the topiary flowers. They are nestled in terra cotta wicker bowls and place
amid a profusion of silver candlestick

Opposite: The clusters of lily-like white agapanthus are mirrored in the bron
ceiling of the bar, where mild hues of brown and dusty pink preva

Preppy Primaries

The three basic brights — red, yellow and blue — are mixed
and matched in these sprayed clay pots. Yellow iris plunge
into tubes of water. The red caladium is cooled down by
the smaller plants, green and white caladium.

Mrs. Matthew Newman

Tulip Vase is the name of the contemporary ceramic sculpted by Betty Woodman.
Yellow tulips bob and weave in graceful trajectories, uninhibited by any other
foliage. The entity contrasts markedly with the Americana surrounding it, including
the banister-back chairs, Fairfield (Conn.), c.1710-1750.

Mrs. Ernest T. Rouse Ir

Left: Coffee for four in the kitchen is enhanced by a yellow enamelware collande
It serves as a container for the centerpiece and holds a tray for some of the pastrie
The tray is covered with galax leaves. The flowers are Marguerite daisie
Top: Baskets of unpeeled wicker hang by ribbons, which in illusion appear to b
stripes removed from the wallpape

Above: A daisy chrysanthemum plant is bedded securely with excelsior in a brow
glazed and spiraled salad bowl. It poses against bright copper molds hanging fro
yellow pegboar

Opposite: Daisies welcome arriving guests. Windows with three shelves each flar
the double entry doors. There are brass cache pots of spider plants and miniatu
liquor bottles filled with Marguerite daisie

Mrs. Margie W. May

A gilded bronze Thai Buddha from the 19th century upstages a 1931 Picasso still life of fruit, bowl and pitcher. Forcing their way to the center of attention, however, are the gerbera daisies in Picasso colors, spotlighted by branches of flowering white crabapple and swirling palmetto leaves.

Mrs. Wallace H. Smith

Vases of snapdragons and variegated ivy pay tribute to a Bar Harbor scene painted
by Wallace H. Smith. A unique collection of French christening boxes drifts atop
the heirloom chest.

Missouri Historical Society

RAYMOND F. PISNEY, DIRECTOR

Above: Magnificent, regal rhododendron blooms and delicate gorgeous single and double peonies adorn the equally magnificent Bixby Bowl

The elaborate sterling silver punch bowl was presented to William K. Bixby in honor of his 49th birthday in 1906, by the Bibliophile Society. The base is decorated with carved Acanthus leaves, while 12 Corinthian columns encircle the top. A frieze of griffins and trophies in 14-caret gold and bibliophilic symbols gild it still more. The bowl is exhibited in the area featuring St. Louis-made furniture, including the clocks shown at left

Mrs. Van C. Parriott

A fragrant greeting stands in the entrance hall.
Carefree garden honeysuckle combined with
California cultivated Queen Anne's lace, grace-
fully twists from a Chinese melon jar, c. 1830.
The display is reflected in a reverse painted
Moroccan mirror of the 1920s.

Mrs. James Rush James J

Above: An assembly of flowers, oversized, y
light and lighthearted, dominates an area between tw
sofas. White delphinium, the veined textured foliag
from croton, red huckleberry, yellow Fantasy rose
deep yellow iris and cream colored love lilies crisscros
their stems in a crystal cylinder vas

Left: A pair of silver wine coolers filled with deep gree
pittosporum foliage are stationed on either side of th
fireplace. In the right background, one of a pair
matching cachepots is filled with coppery daisy mum

Mrs. Sanford N. McDonnell

A dramatic impact results from a daring color scheme — a contemporary treatment for a silver family heirloom vase. The flaring trumpet holds hot pink peonies, blue agapanthus, pink larkspur, lavender crown asters and watermelon-colored carnations. The accents of dripping green are sprengeri fern.

Mrs. Walter F. Ballinger

Lunch for two on moving-in day — it could have been so mundane, but flower
have made it something special. Red and yellow flowers of various shapes an
sizes are water tubed and tucked into a bandana-covered pot of mixed texture
house plants. This is a fun way to say, ''Happy new home!'

Even the mirror-like glaze on the paper lunch bags marks the move to a ne
home as a joyous occasion

St. Louis Magazine

MRS. W. ELLIOT BENOIST
Paper flowers shout out their flamboyant colors — orange, hot pink, lemon yellow
and pumpkin. Their voices are bold and brassy: ''Come look at us!''

A helium filled balloon tugs above a preppy green basket of lemons and blue cornflowers. They were sent to a young, new entrepreneur on his opening day. The card reads, ''Congratulations! May your profits ever go up, and your business never go sour.''

LEMONAID 2¢ GLASS

Mrs. William P. Beavers

May Day is an enchanting and ancient English custom which survives today. It often is celebrated by hanging homemade maybaskets of garden flowers to the door of a friend on the first morning of May. The anonymous donor rings the bell — then runs.

A red wagon carries the makings of the May Day surprise — complete with scissors, woven baskets of construction paper and, of course, lots of spring flowers.

Mr. James A. Van San...

A duet of designs by architect William A. Bernoudy, F.A.I.A.: an urn with pedest
of stainless steel and bronze and the paneled music room where it is stage
Maranta, the Brazilian prayer plant, stays in low key to allow alstroemeria to bla
forth its orange-vermilion colo

Right: The dramatic, almost stark look of dried pussy willow eminates from a floc
vase and fans freely, forming its own desig

The surprise element — from ordinary to extraordinary — is induced here by wayside wilding, Pastinaca sativa (wild parsnip). It takes on airs as it is displayed in a beautifully handpainted German pitcher. The smaller vessel features giant, gaudy and sunny marigolds.

PRIVATE

Mrs. William McBride Love

This garden is in transit — mobile flower boxes of spider plants, Marth
Washington geraniums and sprengeri. When not flower bedecked and o
the go, the private Love car sits sedately at the Museum of Transpor

Mrs. Richard J. Bender

A black tie picnic for four is an unlikely occurrence, but it can happen. At each place setting a black oriental trivit balances a miniature brass pitcher. That in turn offers a single red Samantha rose — a gift to each guest. Black bow ties ring red satin napkins. The flatware is gold and stainless steel. The dinnerware is banded in gold and platinum. The ''table'' is clothed in black and red taffeta with matching seat cushions. The centerpiece is a magnum of Dom Perignon, cooled in brass and illuminated by hurricane lamps of pewter and brass.

Overleaf: The clover-dotted lawn is graced with white astilbe and a picnic basket filled with umbrellas, for rain or for shine.

Mrs. David R. Calhoun

Gigi and Elegance are the names of the petite carnation flowers arranged in a pink wicker breadbasket.

Upper right: This is a closet hanger – white wax begonia blooms, pink sweetheart roses and baby's breath overflow a miniature pink and white polka dotted shopping bag.

Mrs. Edmonstone F. Thompson

A rococco mirror backs a resplendent assemblage of Meissen dinnerware. The soup tureen with platter is mounded with blue hydrangeas, branches of flowering plum lending it height.

Left: In the glittering china cabinet, tea cups brim with pink and red sweetheart roses, pink miniature carnations, more plum branches and the leaves of small red caladium.

Mrs. Miquette Magnus Potter

New blue — a Danish, lifesize columnar lady proudly sports a bonnet of rubrum lilies

Old blue — a collection of Meissen china is enraptured by azalea and cornflowers

Right: The guest bedroom is vernally bright from head to foot where his-and-hers baskets of mixed spring flowers await the visitors

Powell Symphony Hall
St. Louis Symphony Orchestra

LEONARD SLATKIN, MUSIC DIRECTOR & CONDUCTOR
DAVID J. HYSLOP, EXECUTIVE DIRECTOR

Magnificence begets magnificence. One hundred and fifty Samantha roses
musically grace the halls of Powell

Mrs. G. Duncan Bauman

These sparkling embossed vases are heirlooms which have decorated the bridal tables of three generations. They are joined with chains of crystal. Drifts of baby's breath and trails of variegated ivy form the basis of the arrangement. It is punctuated with white roses, because in the Victorian language of flowers they say, "I am worthy of you." Old fashioned love knots symbolize the unity.

An oversized Persian copper container takes on unconventional challenge. It supports a gathering crystal bud vases filled with yellow lilies and deut blooms. A mass of ice cubes coolly conceals the contriv mechanics. The bronze service plates are from Thailar The handsome table and chairs from the original Noond Club have been in the Medart family for many yea

Mrs. Brice R. Smith Jr.

Above: Lunch on deck. A lime wicker basket is stuffed with green bananas, corn on the cob, turnips, eggplant and red cabbage, cut in half to display its inner swirls. Anchored among the edibles are asters from California, blue Exia from Holland and grass gone to seed from a nearby field.

Mr. Wm. Julius Polk Je

Above: Superlative calla lilies arranged with their own foliag
grace a cornucopia from Leerdam, Holland, designed by Andre
Copier. The portrait is of Col. Wm. Polk, a member of Ge
George Washington's staff. Legend says the colonel once caug
a bullet between his teeth

Left: The table is Florentine, inlaid petradura. This is a top view
showing the astonishing skills of the artisans who worked in th
medium of colored ston

Mrs. Donald Danforth Jr.

The view from the top shows a circular table crowned with a king size arrangement of mixed cut foliage encrusted with Limonium bonduelii — yellow statice.

Mrs. Harold E. Thayer

Dancing lady orchids — Oncidium sphacelatum — bloo
bountifully in an unpeeled wicker market basket. It stand
before a portrait of Mr. Thayer by Lou Charno. The antiqu
cherrywood dropleaf harvest table, with square and turne
kitchen legs, dates from 1850. The hall case clock, c.1829,
by Riley Whiting of Winchester, Connecticu

Missouri Botanical Garden

PETER RAVEN, DIRECTOR

There is an emphasis on contrast when American primitive crockware and a barrel are the containers for floral artistry in a Japanese garden. The flowers are all from Missouri roadsides — fleabane and white yarrow, field daisies and thistle. The smooth rocks form a transition between the two cultures, as flowers pay a natural and native tribute to the oriental art form.

Mrs. William A. McDonnell

The flowers glow instead of the candles in the Baccarat and Bristol blue family heirloom lusters. They dominate a background of wallpaper picturing a Japanese hillside. Red clover, Queen Anne's lace, and more cultivated forms such as pink roses and bronze chrysanthemums intermingle with sprengeri and tradescantia foliage. The arrangement shares honor with the shimmering silver of the tea and coffee service.

Mrs. Charles A. Dilt

White wicker baskets resting on either side of the hearth rail swell with wi...
Chinese mustard and wild sweet william. A branch of fresh appleblossom lends i
delicate air to the area over the weather vane above the fireplac

Opposite: In the dining room, an overgrown egg basket holds an effortless array
apple blossoms, ageratum, vinca vines, caladium and lavender streptocarpu

Mrs. Charles A. Thomas

A Dresden lady, more than a century old, stands by a tree trunk forced into bloom with branches of fragrant mock orange. A single Sonia rose floats peacefully in small pond beneath the tree.

The assembly calls to mind the words of Joyce Kilmer: "I think that I shall never see a poem as lovely as a tree."

Mrs. Martin Lammert IV

There's no end to the places for placing flowers. Carnations in sherbet colors
fill a ribbon-tied basket and decorate the mailbox of this remodeled and expanded
farmhouse.

A matching arrangement adorns the front door.

Mrs. Robert B. Smith

Martha Washington geranium blossoms, Maranta with its splotches and Tradescentia with its stripes — all swing from a lantern vase sitting on a slant-top desk.

Left: Reflected in the mirror is a portrait of Wallace H. Smith by St. Louis artist Jane Pettus.

Right: Lime-green dieffenbachia, rooting in a double lipped water bottle, is introduced to the fragrance and charm of Madonna lilies.

Mrs. Cleon O. Swayzee

Above: A thick oval crystal bowl is informally exuberant with phlox, giving the look of lavender lace. Shooting off on tangents are plantlets of Chlorophytum, spider plants.

In the small picture, a summer fireplace arrangement employs an oversize basket to hold a profusion of Sinceri geraniums. The lithograph above the fireplace is by Peter Marcu

The St. Louis Zoo

CHARLES HESSEL, DIRECTOR

Noah's animals marched in two by two, and so do these stuffed animals at the St. Louis Zoo. They are disembarking from a wicker vessel filled with yellow daisies, chrysanthemums, red carnations and cornflowers. Their craft has been held aloft by balloons.

The baleful stare by the animal at left is more than mere curiosity. Seconds after the shutter snapped the arrangement became lunch.

Mrs. Francis D. Seward Jr.

This setting is for a birthday dinner for eight at Busch's Grove, in one of the coz
outdoor huts. A green calico cloth provides the background for balloon-pin
napkins and pink balloons. A miscellany of bottles hold pink garden larkspur

A Few Of My Favorite Things

Here are some personal notes. The pottery mug was made by my son Christian when he was a little boy. He chose his father's favorite color, but presented it with an apology: ''Dad, the eyes fell off.'' The mug is the container for an African violet.

My daughter Martha decorated two utilitarian bottles with tissue paper when she was a child. Each is filled with a single flower, a larkspur.

Our ebullient daughter Sarah created the two ceramic containers while she was in elementary school. The lidded one at left has the single embossed word ''Plant'' on it, so it holds a bird's nest fern. The other bears the embossed legend ''Hi.'' We filled it with cornflowers.